F

KNOW YOUR SELF

A GUIDE TO DISCOVERING THE POWER OF YOUR PERSONALITY.

BASED ON THE WORK OF CARL JUNG.

BY

JOHN VAN DER STEUR

www.powerofpolarities.com
www.polarityconsulting.com

Published by Polarity Institute, Austin, Texas.
The Power of Polarities is a registered trademark (Reg. U.S. Pat. & Tm. Off.).
www.powerofpolarities.com

First Edition, 2018

ISBN: 978-0-9993253-2-2

To Carl Jung, the great pioneer of modern type theory, and to my daughters Eline and Mea, who show me every day how it works.

This book is a Study Guide belonging to:

THE POWER OF POLARITIES

An Innovative Method to Transform Individuals, Teams, and Organizations.
Based on Carl Jung's Theory of the Personality.
By John van der Steur

Free Bonus Materials
Personality Profile and Free Chapter
https://www.powerofpolarities.com/bonusmaterials

CONTENT

Like a painter,
with her palette of colors...

Introduction

Type is fundamental to understanding your motivation, your learning style, the way you communicate, and the way you do your best work.

Your personality contains the raw materials with which you create and shape your personal and professional life. It is like the painter's palette from which you take colors to put on your life's painting.

This book is based on the work of the great Swiss psychologist Carl Jung, who discovered that people's behavior is not random and that besides individual differences between people, there are also typical differences. He called them "psychological types."

These patterns run deep, carving the rivers through which our lives flow. It can explain why one person has the temperament to become a scientist, and another an artist.

To develop our personalities, to become who we are meant to be is a lifelong task. Sooner or later, life compels us to ask ourselves: Who am I? What makes me different? Where do I want to go? How do I get there? A good place to start finding answers to these questions is your personality.

This guide is intended to give you a general introduction and to help you discover the "Spine of the Personality," the relationship between the most conscious and unconscious functions of your personality, so vital for your personal growth and effectiveness.

This book takes some of the core principles of my previous book, *The Power of Polarities.* It presents them in a more accessible and colorful way to help you apply Jung's theory of the personality to your everyday life.

The Spine of the Personality

Chapter 1

The Three Polarities of the Personality

Any experience you have is structured by your mind, specifically by the part we call the personality. It structures information, decisions, and actions. The typical way in which a mind processes information is called a personality type.

Carl Jung observed that besides many individual differences there are also typical differences between people. According to Jung, whose work has been popularized by the MBTI (or Myers-Briggs Type Indicator), a personality is made up of three fundamental polarities that each play a specific role in our personality.

The table below describes each of these polarities and their specific tasks or functions:

Task	***Polarities***	
Perceiving Functions *Gathering information*	**Sensation (S)** *Facts, practical experience, specific details.*	**Intuition (N)** *Imagination, ideas, possibilities, general meaning.*
Judging Functions *Making decisions*	**Thinking (T)** *Causality and logic, objective and impersonal.*	**Feeling (F)** *Compassion and warmth, people and relationships.*
Attitude *Connecting inner and outer world*	**Introversion (I)** *Reflection, quiet, inner orientation, inner standards.*	**Extraversion (E)** *(Inter)action, busy, outer orientation, outer standards.*

It is important to bear the following in mind:

- All three polarities are always present in us.
- There are no right or wrong, good or bad, useful or useless properties.
- How we use them depends on the situation we find ourselves in.

Carl Jung also attributed four colors to the four functions *Sensation, Intuition, Thinking* and *Feeling*:

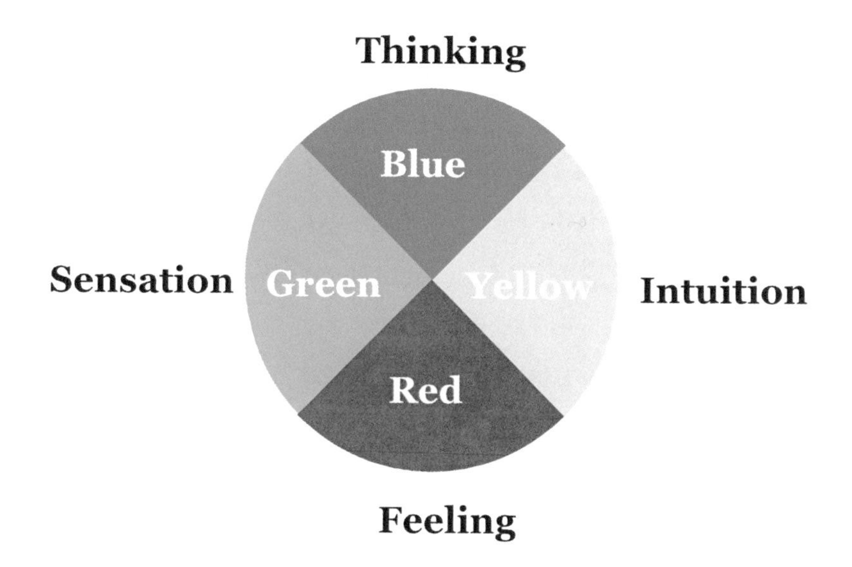

"Feeling is red, this is connected with blood and fire, with passion and love which is supposed to be warm and glowing.
Sensation is green, this is connected with the earth and perceiving reality.
Thinking is white, or blue, cold like snow.
Intuition is gold or yellow because it is felt to shine and radiate."

(C. G. Jung, Modern Psychology: ETH Lectures, Volume 4)

The Perceiving Polarity

Green Sensation – *Yellow Intuition*

The purpose of this polarity is to gather information. One way is through *Green Sensation* which uses the five senses to perceive (Sight, Sound, Smell, Touch and Taste). It is interested in real, verifiable data.

The opposite way is through *Yellow Intuition*, which uses the 6th sense to perceive the world of ideas that are not yet tangible but one day could be. *Yellow Intuition* sees the forest before it sees the trees, *Green Sensation* sees the individual trees before it sees the forest.

Yellow Intuition needs to see the big picture before it can drill down into the details. *Green Sensation* needs to understand all the specifics before it can see the big picture.

An important thing we can learn from this polarity is that everything is really created twice. It is created once in the imagination and once in physical reality.

The Judging Polarity

Blue Thinking – *Red Feeling*

The purpose of this polarity is to make decisions about how we appraise, organize and act on the information we receive from the perceiving functions.

Blue Thinking tends to organize impressions logically in a manner that is impersonal, objective and task oriented. *Blue Thinking* uses the mind to solve complex problems. It analyzes information to find the cause and effect, the consistency and the logical order of things.

Red Feeling on the other hand likes to organize impressions through a personal and more subjective value judgement such as a like or dislike or an appreciation or depreciation. It relies on the heart for its judgements.

When you buy a car with *Blue Thinking*, you will use logical criteria like maintenance records. *Red Feeling*, on the other hand, will look more at color, comfort and whether the sales person is likeable or not.

SUMMARY OF THE FOUR FUNCTIONS

Green Sensation	Factual, precise, practical, detailed, focused on reality of past and present
Yellow Intuition	Imaginative, big picture oriented, focused on potentiality and the future

Blue Thinking	Logical, impersonal, analytical, objective, task and result oriented
Red Feeling	Compassionate, empathic, personal, people and relationship oriented

The Polarity of Orientation
Introversion - Extraversion

The purpose of this polarity is to connect with ourselves and the world around us.

The ***introverted*** attitude is oriented towards the inner world through reflection. The ***extraverted*** attitude is oriented more towards the outer world and likes to interact with it.

We all ***introvert*** and ***extravert*** for longer or shorter periods of time, like we inhale and exhale to breathe. If you feel most alive when you interact with the world around you, you probably are more ***extraverted***. And if you feel most alive and energized when absorbed in your inner world, you are probably more introverted.

Sometimes introversion is not understood so well. Susan Cain, an insightful speaker and author on the power of introversion wrote:

> ***The next time you see a person with a composed face and a soft voice, remember that inside her mind she might be solving an equation, composing a sonnet, designing a hat. She might, that is, be deploying the power of quiet.***

Take a cup for example...

Let's take a cup as a simple example of an everyday situation where all these polarities operate together in our personality.

When we hold a cup in our hands, ***Green Sensation*** tells us that there is a physical object with a particular shape. ***Blue Thinking*** tells us the object is a cup. ***Red Feeling*** tells us whether we like it, whether it is agreeable or not. And ***Yellow Intuition*** tells us the potential of the cup, its possibilities, all the things we can do with it.

With our ***Introversion,*** we reflect on the cup, and with our ***Extraversion,*** we interact with it, we use it. In other words, *we all use all polarities all the time.*

Chapter 2

Preference Makes the Difference

We all use all polarities of the personality all the time. What makes us different is our preference for and conscious use of these polarities. We prefer the poles that we feel most comfortable with, the ones we feel we can trust and rely on the most.

The ones that we prefer are the ones we tend to favor above the others. We use them the most and they develop into a habit and a strength, thus creating a "typical" pattern in our personalities.

Preference makes the difference because it is how we engage with our inner and outer worlds and make our mark on them.

There is a short exercise we can do to illustrate this. Take a moment to cross your arms in front of you...

Now look at your arms. Which arm is on top? Your right or your left? I bet that if you did this 10 times, you'd find that nine out of ten times the same arm would be on top.

And now, try to put the other arm on top. How does this feel, what is this like? Does it feel awkward and strange? Do you struggle doing it?

It is the same in the personality. We have a preference for certain poles over others. What is your preference? ***Sensation*** over ***Intuition***, ***Thinking*** over ***Feeling***? Some functions come more naturally. We are used to applying them. We trust and rely on them more than others.

This doesn't mean we don't have the other ones, but they just aren't as easy for us to access, nor are they as well-developed. The preferred way becomes the favorite and “best way” to accomplish something.

A good method of discerning which poles of a polarity you prefer, is to see how much energy it takes to use that function or attitude.

Is it easy and natural? Does it energize you? Are you drawn to it? Or does it tend to be a struggle, does it drain you of energy, and is it slow, painful, overwhelming and perhaps boring...?

Carl Jung established a naming convention for the order of preference of each of the four functions:

1. ***Dominant function*** (used most)
2. ***Auxiliary function*** (used next)
3. ***Tertiary function*** (used occasionally)
4. ***Inferior function*** (used least)

And he noted the 1st and 4th function are always polar opposites! For example, if ***Red Feeling*** is dominant, then ***Blue Thinking*** will be inferior.

The first three functions are what you use to run your life. You enjoy using them, and you trust and rely on them the most. And hopefully, you have chosen a profession where you get to use them!

The fourth function Jung called “inferior” because it is the least developed, awkward and slow. It is the most unconscious of all the functions and it is where we can become bored, overwhelmed and easily upset. No wonder we try to avoid it in ourselves and others.

The worst thing about the *Inferior function* is that you cannot control or develop it. Instead, it controls and develops you! It develops you by introducing new ways of looking at things and new skills for solving problems. When all the other functions have been exhausted, this is the one that comes to your aid and saves the day.

There is an exercise you can do to determine your order of preference. In the table on the next page, mark the words that apply and appeal most to you. Then count how many words you marked in each column. See which of the functions has the highest score, which is second, third, and fourth.

Perceiving		*Judging*	
Sensation	**Intuition**	**Thinking**	**Feeling**
Factual	Imaginative	Logical	Personal
5 Senses	6th Sense	Head	Heart
Precise	General	Objective	Subjective
Data	Meaning	Analysis	Relationship
Details	Ideas	Problems	Needs
Present	Future	Cause-effect	Value
Proven	Hypothetical	Challenging	Supporting
Concrete	Symbolic	Reason	Empathy
Traditional	Original	Critical	Accepting
Safe	Risky	Tough	Tender
Routine	Variety	Argument	Appreciation
Actuality	Possibility	Discussion	Harmony
Practical	Abstract	Firm	Adaptable
Form	Content	Cool	Warm
Experience	Belief	Criteria	Care
Sensible	Speculative	Intellectual	Aesthetical
What?	Why?	How?	Who?

Tally your counts here:

Sensation	Intuition	Thinking	Feeling

In interpreting your scores, take the following into account: *the 1st and 4th preference are opposite.* In other words, the function that is dominant is determined as much by your highest as by your lowest score. Your strongest preference is determined as much by your like as your dislike.

If for example, you have a high tally for both ***Thinking*** and ***Intuition***, which one is dominant? For this you have to look at the difference with the other functions.

If the difference between ***Thinking*** and ***Feeling*** is highest, then ***Thinking*** is dominant. If the difference between ***Intuition*** and ***Sensation*** is highest, probably ***Intuition*** is your dominant function.

Take a moment to write down the order in which you use your colors here:

1. ___________
2. ___________
3. ___________
4. ___________

Chapter 3

Type and Temperament

The four functions do not act in isolation, they are like notes that like to make music together. They usually act in pairs of perceiving and judging functions. Together they form temperaments: deep underlying typological patterns from which people observe, process information and act.

As such they show up in patterns of (inter)action, talents, needs, values, and roles people play.

The table on the next page shows how the functions team up to produce four distinct temperaments, each with its own color code: ***Technician,*** ***Helper,*** *Inventor* **and** *Visionary.*

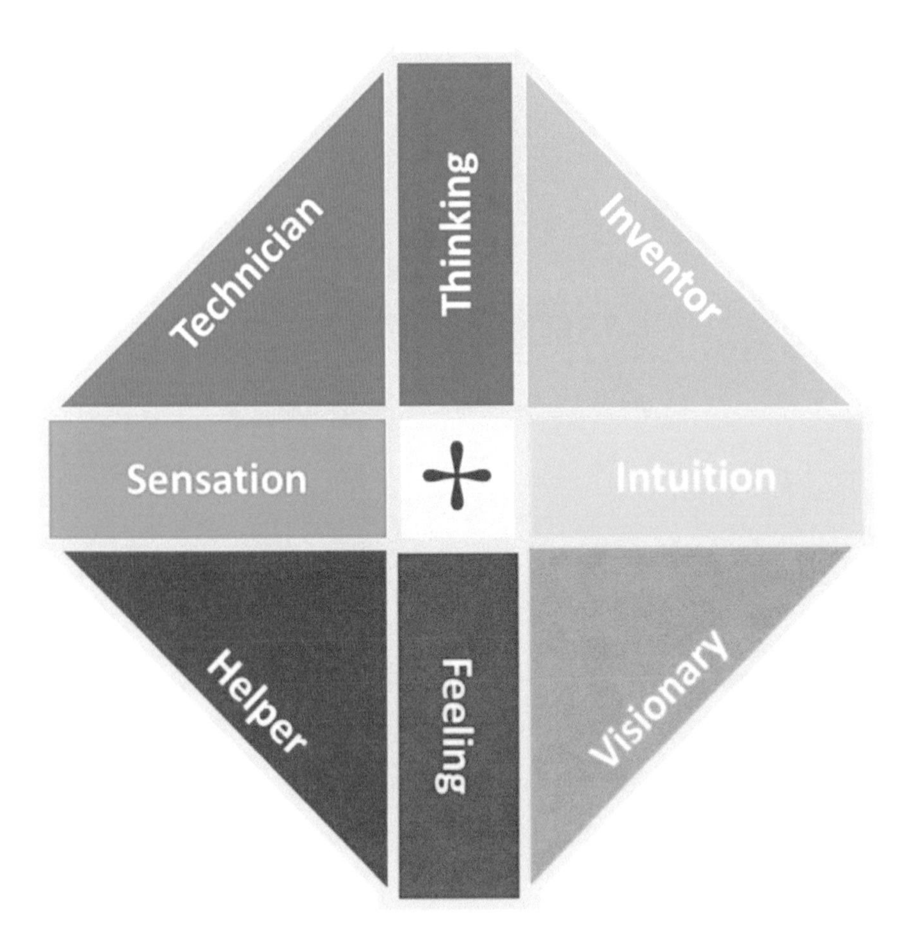

Our worldview is primarily determined by our temperament, i.e., the combination of a perceiving (*Sensation* or *Intuition*) and a judging (***Thinking*** or ***Feeling***) function.

If there are four worldviews, it begs the question, ***"What color is the sky in your world?"***

TEAL Temperament – Technician

People under the ***Teal Sky*** will look for hard, tangible facts and their logical order. They see the world as the result of cause and effect, are highly technical, and are good at establishing rules and procedures. People with this worldview often like to practice law, engineering, or western medicine. A good example is Bill Gates, with his determination to dominate office software through Microsoft. It is the most prevalent worldview in Europe and North America.

TERRACOTTA Temperament – Helper

People under the ***Terracotta Sky*** people will engage with the practical side of reality and will be inclined to see how they affect people. They seek to organize the world in a way that meets human needs, and they strive to help and be of service to others. People with this worldview work in professions like nursing, childcare, education, and hospitality. This temperament is prevalent in certain Asian and South American countries.

ORANGE Temperament – Visionary

People under the *Orange Sky* are oriented towards human principles like love, personal growth, and human rights. They seek to organize the world in ways that help people fulfill their potential. They are interested in creating a new vision for humanity, and can express this poetically, like Martin Luther King in his *"I Have a Dream"* speech or Bob Dylan in a song like "*The Times They Are A-Changin'*." People with this worldview can be found in more idealistic professions like psychology, counseling, religious leadership, writing, poetry, and movies.

TURQUOISE Temperament – Inventor

People under the *Turquoise Sky* are interested in "thought experiments" through which they discover new and exciting ideas that will change the world. They like to make scientific discoveries, or create inventions, innovations, new designs and architectures. People with this worldview like to make the future happen. Like Steve Jobs in technology, Albert Einstein in physics, or Frank Lloyd Wright in architecture.

Under each of these four color skies, things look very different. And yet, when these four skies come together, a creative process takes place with unusual results.

Let's say you want to build a new house. The ***Teal Technician*** will focus on the technical design and completion on time and within budget. The *Turquoise Inventor* will desire to implement new technologies and designs, something ***Teal*** will find too risky. The ***Terracotta Helper*** will want to focus on the people that will live in the house and their practical needs. And the *Orange Visionary* will be dreaming of beauty, of the most marvelous designs, like those of the famous architect Antoni Gaudi which you can see in Barcelona.

Under stress, however, these qualities become overextended and turn into weaknesses. Look at the tables on the next page and take a moment to reflect: *when are you having a good day, and when a bad one?*

The important thing to know about stress behavior is that it is oriented towards *survival* and is never as productive, healthy and effective as "good day behavior".

Having A Good Day...	
Disciplined Precise Practical Efficient Competitive	Original Purposeful Independent Effective Bold
Supportive Kind Dependable Dedicated Caring	Idealistic Encouraging Holistic Inspiring Meaningful

Having A Bad Day...	
Controlling Nitpicking Risk-averse Calculating Ruthless	Unrealistic Detached Argumentative Dominant Narcissistic
Worried Complaining Withdrawn Resentful Smothering	Chaotic Inauthentic Codependent Flighty Insecure

Chapter 4

The Spine of the Personality

What Jung called the Inferior Function is the fourth function of preference, and its key characteristic is that it is unconscious. It is there, always, and you basically have a limited or zero control over it. Instead, it has control over you. Jung called it inferior because it is the least developed, awkward, and slow. It is the capacity in yourself and others that you are the most frustrated with and distrustful of. It is the Achilles Heel of the personality, the "blind spot," the place of the Shakespearean "fatal flaw." It trips you up, makes you stumble, and fall.

A fascinating quality of it is that you cannot develop it. Instead, it develops you! It even comes to your aid in a time of great need. It is the function that is directly connected with the unconscious, which Carl Jung discovered is the source of personal growth, change, and transformation.

If we do not want to be subject to unconscious misfortune, awareness of our fourth preference is at least as important as awareness of our first. It is how we can experience true freedom. Jungian analyst John Beebe calls this the *backbone* of the personality:

> ***When there is development of both the superior and the inferior functions, we can speak of a 'spine' of consciousness that gives a personality backbone.***
>
> (Beebe, 2017, Ch. 8)

There are four possible spines of consciousness. One for each function and its opposite.

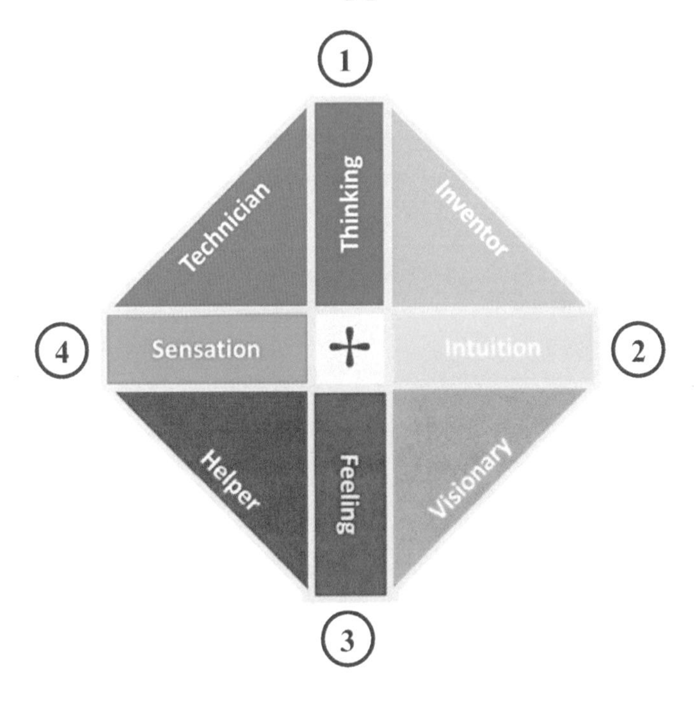

Which one of these four is your spine? Put a checkmark in the column next to it.

	Dominant	***Unconscious***	✓
Spine 1	Blue Thinking	Red Feeling	
Spine 2	Yellow Intuition	Green Sensation	
Spine 3	Red Feeling	Blue Thinking	
Spine 4	Green Sensation	Yellow Intuition	

By developing a strong backbone, you can use your Inferior Function to have a positive, moral, and powerful impact. There is as much positive as negative potential in the shadow.

To discover what gifts a "spine of consciousness" brings, you can find on the next pages an overview of the *conscious* and *unconscious* personality of each of the "spines." There is a description of the qualities and behaviors that are "typical" for each spine.

Conscious means that you are aware of it and can have conscious control over it. Unconscious does not mean you do not have it. You do! You just lack awareness and have limited control over it.

Conscious Personality

E – Extraverted Orientation

Ne	Innovator ENTP	Te	Operator ESTP	Se
N	INVENTOR	T	TECHNICIAN	S
Ni	INTP Architect	Ti	ISTP Investigator	Si

I – Introverted Orientation

Less Conscious & Unconscious Personality

E – Extraverted Orientation

Se	Host ESFP	Fe	Inspirer ENFP	Ne
S	HELPER	F	VISIONARY	N
Si	ISFP Caregiver	Fi	INFP Poet	Ni

I – Introverted Orientation

Spine 1: Blue Thinking Dominant

The *conscious personality* (left page) represents the qualities this type has conscious control over and are relatively well developed. The unconscious personality (left page below) is more difficult to access and develop.

Spine	**Blue Thinking - Red Feeling**
Quality	Strong sense of clear, logical order.
Support	**Sensation - Intuition**
Temper-aments	**Teal Technician - Turquoise Inventor**
Motto	"Every person needs a plan and needs to stick to it!"
Pitfall	Finds it hard to show affection, empathy, and compassion.
Negative Judgement of Opposite	Feeling is soft, touchy and feely! Please no Kumbaya! Being soft is not only dangerous, but weak!
Dark Shadow	Establishes sudden, irrational and extreme loyalties that can be kept secret and be very destructive.
Redeeming Shadow	Truly love yourself and your neighbor, and be aware of irrational and extreme loyalties or commitments.

Conscious Personality

E – Extraverted Orientation

Fe	Inspirer ENFP	Ne	Innovator ENTP	Te
F	VISIONARY	N	INVENTOR	T
Fi	INFP Poet	Ni	INTP Architect	Ti

I – Introverted Orientation

Less Conscious & Unconscious Personality

E – Extraverted Orientation

Te	Operator ESTP	Se	Host ESFP	Fe
T	TECHNICIAN	S	HELPER	F
Ti	ISTP Investigator	Si	ISFP Caregiver	Fi

I – Introverted Orientation

Spine 2: Yellow Intuition Dominant

The conscious personality (left page) represents the qualities this type has conscious control over and are relatively well developed. The unconscious personality (left page below) is more difficult to access and develop.

Spine	**Intuition - Sensation**
Quality	Uncanny sense of the unknown, the unborn possibilities.
Support	**Thinking - Feeling**
Temper-ament	**Orange Visionary - Turquoise Inventor**
Motto	"I smell a rat" or "I smell a great opportunity"
Pitfall	A good story is better than reality.
Negative Judgement of Opposite	Sensation provides TMI! It is stuck in irrelevant and unimportant details of the past.
Dark Shadow	Sows plentifully but does not reap. Unpunctual and vague. Unhealthy physical habits.
Redeeming Shadow	Pay attention to body, to nature, to housekeeping. Do reality checks on a daily basis. Care for a physical object.

Conscious Personality

E – Extraverted Orientation

Se	Host ESFP	Fe	Inspirer ENFP	Ne
S	HELPER	F	VISIONARY	N
Si	ISFP Caregiver	Fi	INFP Poet	Ni

I – Introverted Orientation

Less Conscious & Unconscious Personality

E – Extraverted Orientation

Ne	Innovator ENTP	Te	Operator ESTP	Se
N	INVENTOR	T	TECHNICIAN	S
Ni	INTP Architect	Ti	ISTP Investigator	Si

I – Introverted Orientation

Spine 3: Red Feeling Dominant

The conscious personality (left page above) represents the qualities this type has conscious control over and are relatively well developed. The unconscious personality (left page below) is more difficult to access and develop.

Spine	**Red Feeling - Blue Thinking**
Quality	To appreciate, value, relate and harmonize.
Support	**Sensation - Intuition**
Temper-aments	**Orange Visionary - Terracotta Helper**
Motto	"We live and work together in harmony."
Pitfall	Selling out to an established system of thought.
Negative Judgement of Opposite	Thinking is cold, critical and cruel. It disrespects and abuses people. It is dehumanizing!
Dark Shadow	Negative about others or society. Selfish, angry, cold and distant.
Redeeming Shadow	Examine negative thoughts and think things through positively.

Conscious Personality

E – Extraverted Orientation

Te	Operator ESTP	Se	Host ESFP	Fe
T	TECHNICIAN	S	HELPER	F
Ti	ISTP Investigator	Si	ISFP Caregiver	Fi

I – Introverted Orientation

Less Conscious & Unconscious Personality

E – Extraverted Orientation

Fe	Inspirer ENFP	Ne	Innovator ENTP	Te
F	VISIONARY	N	INVENTOR	T
Fi	INFP Poet	Ni	INTP Architect	Ti

I – Introverted Orientation

Spine 4: Green Sensation Dominant

The conscious personality (left page above) represents the qualities this type has conscious control over and are relatively well developed. The unconscious personality (left page below) is more difficult to access and develop.

Spine	Green Sensation - Yellow Intuition
Quality	Concrete and practical sense of reality, gets things done.
Support	**Blue Thinking - Red Feeling**
Temper-aments	**Terracotta Helper – Teal Technician**
Motto	"Stick to the facts and get it done."
Pitfall	Thinks what has been always will be (or at least should be).
Negative Judgement of Opposite	Intuition is mad fantasy, has no value what so ever and above all… it is dangerous!
Dark Shadow	Dark premonitions of the future, thoughts of doom, pessimism.
Redeeming Shadow	Embrace a new idea and look for what could be positive in the new and unknown.

Where to go from here...

Jung's theory of the personality is most valuable when you apply it to your own life. There it can facilitate your growth and transformation.

If you have not done so yet, please take a moment to go to our online personality inventory: https://polaritylearning.com/form.html

When you have your profile, reflect on it using the following questions:

- *What are practical examples of how I use my dominant function and my two conscious temperaments?*
- *How effective is my use of them? What are examples?*
- *How could I use them even more effectively?*
- *What are practical examples of my difficulties with my polar opposite, i.e. my 4th inferior function?*
- *How could my 4th function help me be more effective?*
- *If I had to choose one thing to do differently from now on, what would it be?*

Every journey of 1000 miles begins with the first step. Congratulations on taking the step of reading this book and learning about your personality. May you have good fortune on the life long journey of self-discovery!

Know Your Self, Understand Others

You can use the grid below to mark your position and that of significant others in your life. It can help you examine the differences and similarities you have them.

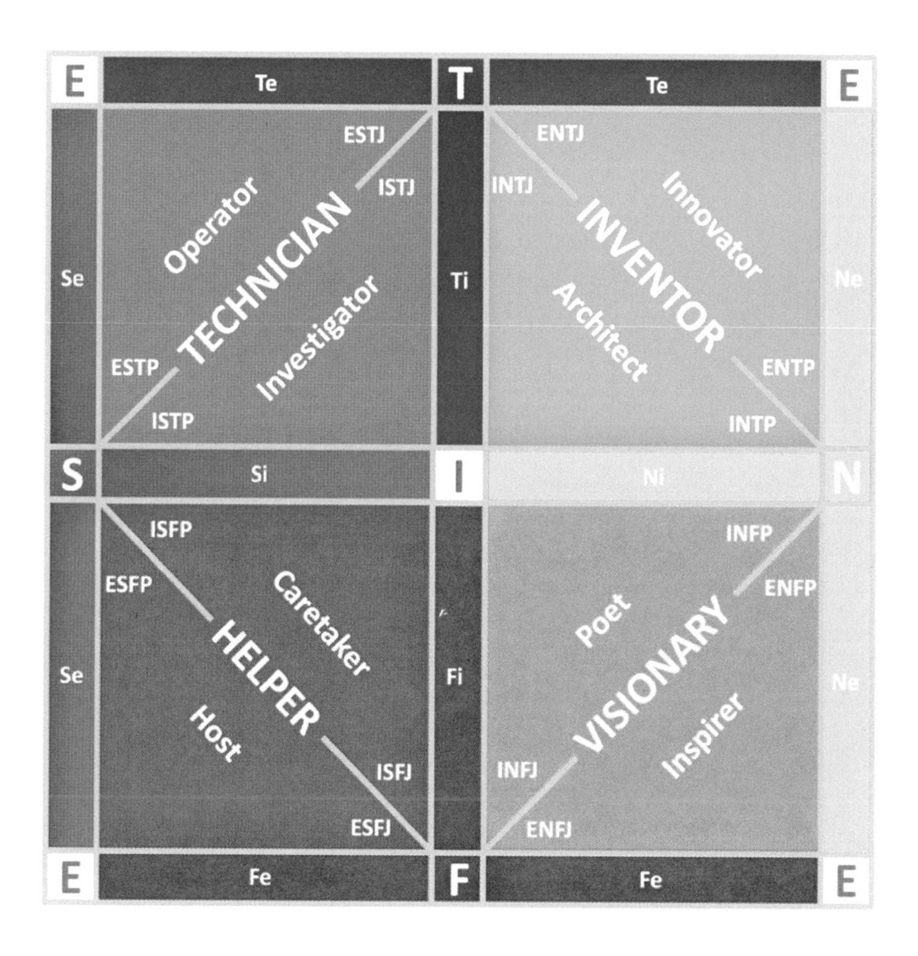

The Power of Polarities Personality Grid™

Summary of "The Power of Polarities"

Polarities are real, and they are everywhere: Light-Dark, Ebb-Flow, High-Low, In-Out, Rest-Movement, Hot-Cold.

One of the great paradoxes of life is that the purpose of polarities is not to polarize, but to harmonize.

There exists in our world an illusion of power. The illusion is that one pole of a polarity is better than the other:

- One right, the other wrong
- One good, the other bad
- One strong, the other weak

This approach is destructive. It leads to division, conflict and instability:

"A house divided against itself, cannot stand"

The value of the psychology of Carl Jung is that it is a psychology of polarities. *"Life is born of the spark of opposites."*, he wrote.

Where can we find what unites polarities, what holds them together? The answer is: *in our center.*

Who are we if we do not know our center? There has never been, nor will there ever be another you.

Your center is where you find your purpose and where your life becomes a unique and authentic act of being and service to mankind. It is the unity that that transcends the diversity of your personality.

Without this center, transformation cannot take place. It is where the polarities of the personality lose their autonomy, let go of their self-centeredness and become connected to the greater whole of your being.

Aligning your personality with your purpose is what this work is all about. This takes place in four essential steps:

1. **Know Your Self**
2. **Understand Others**
3. **Define your Purpose**
4. **Execute: *Live, Love, Learn and Laugh***

"Every advance, every achievement of mankind, has been connected with an advance in self-awareness." ~ Carl Jung

ABOUT THE AUTHOR

John van der Steur grew up in the Netherlands. He attended Pomona College in California as a Fulbright Scholar and has a graduate degree in Economics from the University of Amsterdam.

He has worked with thousands of individuals and hundreds of teams to help them achieve their goals. Clients include corporate teams and Olympic gold medalists. John is also a member of the Association of Psychological Type International and he is a faculty member on the Jung Platform.

In his own words:

"I have had a lifelong fascination with the psychology of Carl Jung and have specialized myself in the practical application of his work. I have experienced how it can change outcomes and even change lives. I am passionate about helping people discover their personalities and see what unique capabilities they bring to the table. This book is the result of 30 years of experience in this field.

I believe you must know yourself if you want to navigate and thrive in today's chaotic world. Understanding your personality, your mind, your heart and most importantly your unique purpose or calling in this world.

I am the product of a Dutch father and an American mother and was raised in the Netherlands. Currently, I live in Austin and am the proud father of two tall Dutch-American girls age ten and twelve."

Made in the USA
Middletown, DE
14 September 2022

10497932R00027